GOD Needs More Annas
A Woman's Guide to Fulfilling Her Purpose

Viveca C. Merritt

DEDICATION

Love to My Daughters, Granddaughters, and Women Everywhere of all Ages who know JESUS Christ as Savior and Lord!

TABLE OF CONTENTS

DEDICATION

FOREWORD

My Personal Invitation

About the Author

FOREWORD

The decade of the nineties has been defined by many as the century of promiscuity, rebellion, self-centeredness, and the list goes on. Surely, by now, we have realized that the Body of Christ is not exempt from such behavior. When a believer becomes born-again and is initially filled with the Spirit of God, he or she is not automatically free from past temptations or habits.

Therefore, it is critical that the Body of Christ have their minds renewed with the Word of God so as to implement new habits, such as praying and fasting.

I believe that the primary area that the devil attacks women in is their identity. Most women—even in Church—are full of insecurity, because they do not know who they are in Christ, nor do they have an accurate vision of what the woman of God should look like or how God expects her to behave.

GOD NEEDS MORE ANNAS will provide women with an ideal model of a true, godly woman. It is my intention to provide you with helpful insight on the lifestyle of a virtuous woman.

This book is for all women—whether married, single, divorced, widowed, or single parent. No matter what your present state-of-being, Jesus will meet you where you are.

Men, I have not forgotten you in this book. If you are single or believing God for a wife, you especially need to read this book. If that special someone does not possess the character of a godly woman, it may be back to the prayer closet for you. Married men should also take note. Be sure that you are doing what is necessary to direct your wives in leading a godly lifestyle.

God Needs More Annas is a book full of practical instructions for the woman of God. It is a book packed with "the basics." I believe that if we, as women of God, would master the basics—prayer, fasting and devotion, then we will experience the fullness of God in our lives.

CHAPTER ONE
Womanhood – Key to a Righteous Society

The purpose of this book is not to give a history lesson on Anna, but to use what the Bible says about her character and women in general as a guide for godly women today. So, before we explore the characteristics of Anna, who was an impeccable example for women. We must examine who woman is, her purpose, and the characteristics of an ungodly and godly woman. This will enable you to understand the value of possessing Anna's character traits. You will also realize that even against the norm or flow of society, you can maintain a holy lifestyle as a woman.

If you examine historical records you will find that men and nations have always been influenced by women. Women have either provided men and nations with a positive or negative influence—what an awesome responsibility we have in the fulfillment of the will of God in the earth! God has ordained that we be women of God—living holy, consecrated, dedicated lives, committed to His Word.

The Bible testifies of Anna as a godly woman who fulfilled her purpose, which was to be used as a vessel to pray continually for Israel and bless the baby Jesus in the temple. As the people of her day watched her go to the temple daily, she must have suffered persecution, but truly her testimony was, "The Lord is my God." I also want my testimony, that truly the Lord is my God, to be apparent to everyone with whom I have contact: my husband, my children, and all others.

If you are in the Body of Christ, it is because God has a plan and a purpose for your life. You are significant to God. He gave His only begotten Son for you, who died that you might have life. You are somebody! Although the world stereotypically views women as difficult, moody, or insignificant, God has ordained us for a purpose. However, walking in purpose involves incorporating God's Word into your life at every turn. You must allow the Holy Spirit to lead and guide you.

I want you to know that God loves you, Jesus loves you, and I love you, however Jesus said in John 14:15, *"If you love me, then keep my commandments."* Love is more than just saying, "I love you," it involves action.

I believe that together we can fulfill the plan and purpose that God has ordained for our lives in this generation, just as Anna did during her time on earth. Anna was a woman of God, who recognized what price she was required by God to pay to fulfill His plan for her life. She was a woman who responded according to her desire to be a vessel of honor, rather than to the dictates of society.

Again, the calling of God demands that you put the Word of God to use daily. You must purpose in your heart to be a doer of the Word. Only then will you be able to discern that which is good from that which is evil; it is called the law of use.

"But strong meat belongeth to them that are of full age, even those who by reason of use have their senses exercised to discern both good and evil." (Hebrews 5:14)

I know some of you might say, "I do not know what God's will is for me, I have been praying and asking Him." But I am telling you, He wants you to develop the discretion and character of a godly woman, through a relationship with your Lord Jesus Christ by the Holy Spirit. As you do this, God will prepare you and bring you into your purpose.

There are various types of women in the Bible, all with different character traits. Therefore, in order for us to obtain an understanding of God's purpose for women, we are to read (study) the Bible instead of Glamour, Cosmopolitan, and Vogue magazines.

Women have always played a significant role in humanity—primarily to complete it. Therefore, if the Church and women in particular are to bring Jesus Christ to the masses, we must stand firm in the laws of God. We must present the standard that God has given us.

God said in Genesis 2:18, *"...It is not good that the man should be alone..."* Since God is the Creator of both male and female, He knew what it would take for man to be able to complete His plan, design, will and purpose for humanity. He knew that man would need someone to help him.

Women are not to be man's 'help meet' as we commonly view the term.—his helper, someone who is subservient. "Help meet" means a helper that is suitable for the other person. There are two separate issues that are addressed here, one of help and the other of suitability. Most of us put the two words together, but the Bible separates the term "help meet" in Genesis 2:20, which means "help fit for the man." We are to be helpers fit for the man, therefore, complementing him.

In complementing the man, women are on the same level, but they are different. We make a unique, essential contribution to a man where he cannot totally be who he is without us. Male and female make up mankind. It is only when each part is functioning to its full capacity that you see what was in the heart of God when He created man.

So, God was saying in Genesis, chapter two, "I am going to make a woman who is suitable for Adam," and that is exactly what He did. He took from the rib, out of the center of Adam's being, and created woman.

God designed Eve to be suitable for Adam, someone who would help him complete the plan that He had ordained for man. Woman made it possible for man to realize his human potential and with her companionship, she would be able to complete the human family through reproduction. I believe God knew exactly what He was doing when He created woman. That is why it is essential that we flow in the office of womanhood to which God has ordained for us.

"So God created man in his own image, in the image of God created he him; male and female created he them. And God blessed them, and God said unto them, Be fruitful, and multiply, and replenish the earth, and subdue it: and have dominion over the fish of the sea, and over the fowl of the air, and over every living thing that moveth upon the earth." (Genesis 1:27-28)

It has always been God's ordained plan that He have a people who are called by His name. He created both male and female with the intent of them being fruitful and multiplying, forming a godly lineage. As a result of man's fall, God had to have another plan: Jesus Christ coming into the world, dying for our sins. Men and women must recognize that they are sinners, therefore, they have to return to God through Jesus Christ. It has always been God's plan that the woman be a helper suitable for man's needs. Woman was created to complete God's plan.

We find in history, particularly in ancient times, that the world has been male dominated. However, if we examine the lives of the women of Israel we will discover that they enjoyed a status not experienced by the surrounding cultures. This was true because the Jews had the law of Moses, God's Word. God gave worth to women, causing them to be held in high esteem, honor, and affection.

Today, we have Jesus Christ. He has already come, died, been resurrected by God the Father, and paid the penalty for sin, causing us to enjoy the freedom of womanhood wherever we go. Woman is esteemed as man's love, companion, confidant, better half, and completion when the Word of God is obeyed, causing the eyes of people's understanding to be enlightened that they may know the truth.

We know that Eve, a woman, was first to transgress God's Word, but it was also through a woman that the Lord Jesus Christ was born, who was God passing through the womb of a woman bringing redemption to the world and Israel. You must understand that you are somebody to God. You have an ordained place in the kingdom of God. God wants you to take that rightful place, but you must do it His way—not your own way, not the way you think, or the way your mother told you to do it, or your grandparent's way, and especially not the world's way. You are to operate according to the pattern God has outlined in His Word.

In my reading and studying about women, I found that in the Old Testament it does say that a woman was her husband's property and that she owed him absolute loyalty. That is what God established in His Word so that women would have their rightful place, not to bring women down. We do read that women called their husbands "lord and master" because they were the head of the homes. They recognized that, if they would respond according to the Word of God rather than their feelings, they would be blessed. They would have their rightful place in society, high esteem and honor if they functioned according to the Word of God.

You do not have to be ashamed to walk according to the Word of God. You do not have to be upset and confused about the Word of God. God has given us His Word and His Spirit that we may be doers of His Word and He expects just that.

Again, because of women, men and nations have been influenced; it is up to us to provide godly influence. As I was meditating on that the Lord said to me, "Do you think that if women stopped going to bars, that the men would continue to go there?" I do not think so. He said, "Do you think that if the women stopped walking the streets and presenting themselves as enticing that the men would go there?" He said, "No Vickey, they wouldn't" He elaborated, "Even in today's bars with happy hour, the motive is to go find someone." I know that there are Christians who do to bars and order 'virgin' drinks, because God told me they do, but the contents of the drink does not justify them being there, because their motive for going is wrong.

God wants you to stay in your rightful place, and not go out seeking, unless it is seeking Him. We must first seek God and His kingdom.

"But seek ye first the kingdom of God, and his righteousness; and all these things shall be added unto you." (Matthew 6:33)

You must seek Him, but that only comes about as you spend time with Him in fellowship. Anna's relationship with God is a perfect example to glean from. Maintaining a quality prayer life is the only way you are going to find out God's perfect will for you.

We see in the history of Israel that when there was a decline in women it was because of the influence of pagan cultures surrounding them. They influenced women's philosophy, customs, as well as their family and marital practices, which is exactly what we are seeing today. Women, for the most part, no longer honor and reverence their husbands as God desires.

In the latter part of the book of Ephesians chapter five, it talks about the relationship between wives and husbands. It states that wives are to submit to their husbands as to the Lord and that the husbands are to be head of the wives as Christ is the head of the Church.

Ephesians 5:28 says, *"So ought men to love their wives as their own bodies. He that loveth his wife loveth himself."*

Verse 33 says, *"...and the wife see that she reverence her husband."*

The word "reverence" means "to feel a deep respect," which is mixed with love, wonder, or fear for someone. If you look up the word "reverence" in the Strong's Bible Concordance, it means "to be terrified, frightened, and afraid." One would think, "Well, am I supposed to be terrified, frightened, and afraid of my husband?" What God desires to show us in this Scripture concerning reverence is that we should be afraid or frightened to do anything against God's will, or that would be displeasing to our husbands. So, as you look at it in this light, the husband is to be the head of the wife and the wife is to submit to the husband. She is to respect him with a deep respect, to have reverence for him, because as she does this, she is operating according to what God has outlined in His Word.

The woman, therefore, is not to do anything to cause God to be ashamed of her or to disgrace God. The wife is to have a deep respect or a reverential fear for her husband because her main goal is to do those things that will please him. She is not going to want to nag him, nor is she going to want to cause him any shame or disgrace, but she is going to reverence him, and she is going to love him with the highest love that a wife can have for husband.

It takes faith for a wife to fulfill her calling just as it does for anything else concerning God. The Bible says that, *"...without faith it is impossible to please him..."* (Hebrews 11:6). A common response of wives to what God has prescribed for them in the Word is, "Well, what about me, who is going to please me?" We must trust that God knows how to meet our needs. If we just allow the Holy Spirit to enlighten our hearts and cause us to understand what He is saying, we can create beautiful marriages. That is what God has purposed for His family, the God-kind of marriages.

The world will try to influence you to do things their way, but we know, through God's Word, that the world's way is the opposite of God's way. Even though we may be Christians, if we have a carnal mind, we are at enmity against God, we are hostile towards God, which means we do not want to obey His Word.

"Because the carnal mind is enmity against God: for it is not subject to the law of God, neither indeed can be." (Romans 8:7)

God does not want you to conform to the world. He said, *"Do not be conformed to this world, but be ye transformed..."* (Romans 12:2). He wants you to change. You must change in order to bring Him glory and honor. You must break out of the mode that the world has set for you and be transformed *"...by the renewing of your mind that you may prove the good, acceptable, and perfect will of God"* (Romans 12:2). However, this is not an automatic process, it takes a quality decision on your part as an act of your will.

Women, we have a place in God and it is up to us to walk in the Word, allowing the Holy Spirit to have pre-eminence in our lives. We must allow Him to rule our lives as opposed to our feelings, upbringing, or any other influences that conflict with the Word of God. He wants us to change and walk according to His ways, then He can promote us to the place He desires for us to be.

Living in times that are critical as the times we live in, we cannot afford to fail to provide the godly influence this society so desperately needs. We can tip the scale either way. God has entrusted is with the keys to a righteous society. We can no longer respond to worldly influences, our upbringing, or the way we feel our husbands are treating us; we must trust God and respond to His Word. Then will we be used by God as vessels to influence our husbands and the world.

CHAPTER TWO
The Ungodly Woman

The Bible depicts certain character traits in women which parallel that of today's women. Names may be different, home lives, and environments may differ, but women are still the same species that God originally created. He knows that you are unique, but He has a prescribed purpose for you.

The Book of Proverbs talks about the different types of women in society. I would like to expound on the negative, then positive descriptive terms used in Proverbs. It talks about the foolish clamorous, strange, evil, whorish, brawling, contentious, and adulterous women.

It would be beneficial if all mothers reading this book (or even those who have some type of influence over young girls) would read through Proverbs with young women, so they may know what thus saith the Lord.

In Proverbs it talks about the foolish woman being clamorous and when you look up the word "foolish" it means "self-confident, believing in one's own ability and power." Therefore, you know if someone is self-confident or believing that they are making it as a result of their own ability, as common day society dictates, then that is not of God. We cannot fulfill God's will for our lives without His power and guidance. If a foolish woman is "clamorous," that means she is making noise, she may be zealously expressing certain feelings or thoughts, but because of the content of her message, it amounts to mere noise.

A foolish woman is one who says, "I can do this without your help, I do not need you..." and yet that is not what God has said in His Word. We need each other! If she is married, she needs her husband and her husband needs her. Therefore, women cannot afford to be foolish or think that they can make it on their own, because God has already said, *"...for without me ye can do anything..."* (John 15:5). Women must realize this and they must not allow others to negatively influence them, especially if they are speaking against the foundational truths in God's Word.

Even the women who are single parents in the Body of Christ and are managing without a husband are not making it on their own. They must realize that Jesus is their source. He will cause their companionship needs to be met. He will show them how to treat their children so that the children will not have a void in their lives.

The only way single parents can follow such a lifestyle is if they allow Jesus to meet those needs, which is accomplished through prayer, fasting, and regularly attending an anointed church. Within her local assembly, there may be a gentleman who would volunteer to take her children and plan activities with them. However, this must be done under extreme caution by the leading of the Holy Spirit and Jesus will fulfill the needs. Therefore, even single mothers can live a happy, joyous life, because Jesus is the head of their lives.

The first chapter of Proverbs talks about wisdom. We know that the fear of the Lord is the beginning of wisdom.

"The fear of the Lord is the beginning of knowledge: but fools despise wisdom and instructions." (Proverbs 1:7)

Not only to fear the Lord, but to trust in Him is also wisdom. You must put your trust in Him, but trust is only developed through a relationship.

When you spend time with the Lord on a daily basis, you will learn to trust in Him. He will walk you through trials, tribulations, and persecutions. He will take you through the abuse and eradicate the emotional wounds of the past, He will say, *"remember them no more."* He declares, when you come to Me you are a new creature, so walk as a new creature (2 Corinthians 5:17). This means you must get your mind in agreement with the Word of God which takes effort. It is necessary in order for you to be the godly woman that God has ordained for you to be.

In Proverbs, chapter two, Solomon is explaining to the men about being delivered from the *"strange woman, even from the stranger which flattereth with her words."* These are seductive women who are enticing, calling after men, seeking and pursuing them. That is not God's way and He does not desire that His precious daughters conduct themselves that way.   These women say, "Oh, I just cannot help myself!" Yes, you can! God has given you His Spirit.

Whenever the Book of Proverbs mentioned a "strange woman," it was referring to an adulteress woman or the other woman, who is a stranger or an alien, which means she did not have a covenant relationship with Jehovah God. She was doing her own thing, allowing her culture or the people around her to influence her. This "strange woman" was not submissive to the Word of God, so they spoke of a stranger as an "adulterous woman or the other woman." This was a warning to the young women to flee from, not to allow themselves to be around strange women. Involvement with strange women would lead them away from God.

An "evil woman" was considered just a "bad woman," who did not submit to the Word of God. She was someone was practiced bad things which was anything contrary to the Word of God.

Also stated in Proverbs was the "whorish woman,"— which meant she committed fornication. She would lead young men astray into her house and influence them to go against God's Word. Men, as well as women are to keep themselves virtuous. They are to be under the covenant of God, therefore, if they have a relationship with God, they are going to practice obedience.

God has stated in His Word, *"For this is the will of God, even your sanctification, that ye should abstain from fornication,"* (1 Thessalonians 4:3).

Men and women who are born again must learn to buffet their flesh or beat it as Paul says, bringing it under subjection to the Word of God. It is a matter of choice, you must make a decision, "Yes, I am going to obey God's Word." If God says, *"Do not commit fornication,"* that means I must pray and fast. I must learn how to bring my body under subjection to the

Word of God in that area, and I must not associate with people who are fornicating.

If you associate with people who are committing fornication, you are going to do the same. The Bible says, *"Be not deceived: evil communications corrupt good manners,"* (1 Corinthians 15:33). "Evil" means an evil lifestyle, or speaks of someone who is doing things that are contrary to the Word of God. "Communications" is allowing them to be your friends and spending quality time with them. If you do this, their influence will begin to erode your resistance and you will eventually do the same things that they do.

"Be ye not unequally yoked together with unbelievers: for what fellowship hath righteousness with unrighteousness? And what communion hath light with darkness?

Wherefore come out from among them, and be ye separate, saith the Lord, and touch not the unclean thing; and I will receive you." (2 Corinthians 6:14, 17)

Even though we live in a modern society, God's Word never changes. Remember, God is the Creator, He knew that we would be living on the earth today. He knew what the condition of the world and society would be, yet He says in His Word that if we allow the Holy Spirit to rule, we can walk in the Spirit and not fulfill the lust of the flesh, which includes committing fornication.

It is possible for a single person to live a content life in Christ, but it takes work. You cannot just assume that because you are born-again and Spirit-filled that you are exempt from temptations. Some people even teach that the Holy Spirit will not allow you to do anything against God's Word. If you allow it, flesh will rule over the Greater One within you. Your flesh will rule over your spirit, even if it has been recreated in the image and likeness of God. Your spirit wants to be led by the Holy Spirit, but if you don't allow Him to rule, your flesh is going to rule.

Proverbs also talks about a wife who is "quarrelsome" in chapter 19, verse 13. The word "brawling" refers to someone who is in strife, one who is prone to arguing or disputing. If a wife is quarrelsome, according to that Scripture, she is a like a *"...continuous dripping."* Everyone knows that a water faucet that continuously drips is very annoying. A wife should not desire to be a brawling or contentious woman as the Scriptures describe.

A "contentious" woman is also one who is in strife and is always quarrelsome. What husband wants to be with a wife who is always nagging, complaining, and murmuring? The Bible speaks against murmurers, complainers, and quarrelsome people in Jude, verse 16. They do not trust Him, they do not believe His Word. God cannot do anything with a wife who exhibits this mannerism, because she is always thinking about her needs, her trust and confidence is not in Jehovah God, the Most High.

Proverbs also talks about the "adulterous women" (a strange woman) whose words are soothing, full of flattery and hypocrisy. It says her lips *"...drop as a honeycomb, and her mouth is smoother than oil. But her end is bitter as wormwood, sharp as a two-edged sword. Her feet go down to death, her steps take hold of hell,"* (Proverbs 5:3-5). This tends to be a married woman who is not in a covenant relationship with her God and she leads other men astray which causes her life to be something other than what God has ordained for it to be.

An adulterous woman entices men to come spend time with her, but Proverbs speaks against these type of women and instructs young me to stay away. If they see her coming, they are to run the other way. A relationship with an adulterous woman may be joyful or pleasurable for a little while, but there is death in the end.

The Scripture also speaks about the husband of the adulterous woman. It says that when he finds out he is going to be in a rage against the man who allowed himself to be enticed by her (Proverbs 6:32-35); it is a no win situation.

Proverbs 2:17 says, *"Which forsaketh the guide of her youth, and forgetteth the covenant of her God."* She forsakes the "guide," the "leader of chief," of her youth. Who was the leader of her youth? It was either her father, husband, or the man of God. It goes on to say and *"...forgetteth the covenant of her God."* These women who walk not according to the Word of God have forsaken the guide of their youth and have forgotten the covenant of their God. That is the reason for their sinful, self-destructive behavior.

Women and men must be very careful about their feelings and emotions. If a wife's needs are not met in the home, she is probably going to go out looking. She has to be very careful. Even if her husband is not meeting her needs, she must have a relationship with the Lord Jesus Christ. This is also true for husbands. Even in the Church we find that men and women are searching for someone to meet their emotional needs, if they are not being met at home, but such behavior is not condoned by God. This is not His will concerning relationships between husbands and wives.

We know that there are plenty of marriages that are not the God-kind of marriages. However, if the individual who is hurting in that marriage would establish a prayer life and a close, intimate relationship with the Lord Jesus Christ, Jesus will fill the void in that person's life. If the wife is submissive to the Lord Jesus Christ and the Holy Spirit, the Greater One within her will teach her how to overcome in that particular marriage. She will not have to go looking for other men to meet those emotional needs.

A woman always enjoys being told that she is pretty, and that she can meet her husband's needs. If she doesn't hear it from her husband, she is going to want to hear it from someone else. She may be led astray to be an adulteress, but that is not God's plan. God's way is to submit to His Word, even if your husband is not meeting your needs, Jesus Christ wants to meet that need in your life. He will show you how you can beautify yourself inwardly, so that you can draw your husband to want to love, cherish and nourish you.

"But ye shall receive power, after that the Holy Ghost is come upon you: and ye shall be witnesses unto me..." (Acts 1:8)

Witnesses here means, "to live a life according to the Word of God," but you must make a decision. He has made us free-will, moral agents. We have the freedom of choice—we can either walk in His Word and be blessed or walk outside of His Word, which means doing our own thing or conforming to the world and be cursed. It is either blessings or cursings—there is no in-between. It is only through the power of the Holy Ghost that a woman can submit to the will of Jesus Christ. Through operating in the power of the Holy Ghost, women can choose to be godly and not fulfill the lusts of the flesh.

GOD Needs More Annas

CHAPTER THREE
Flowing in True Womanhood

The characteristics of a godly, virtuous woman is described in the book of Proverbs. The word of "virtuous" means "force" or "strength" of mind and body is to have fellowship with God, walking according to His Word—being full of the Spirit. To be full of the Spirit means you must pray in the Spirit, being edified by the Holy Spirit. Then you can walk as a godly woman.

Proverbs 12:4 says, *"A virtuous woman is a crown to her husband, but she that maketh ashamed is as rottenness in his bones."* Remember virtuous means "force or strength of mind and body," women who are strong in the Lord, and not in themselves. A wife who rests in the Lord and walks in His Word is *"...a crown to her husband..."*

If you were to run the reference on Proverbs 12:4, to 1 Corinthians 11:7, it reads: *"For a man indeed ought not to cover his head, forasmuch as he is the image and glory of God ..."* The man represents the glory of God or the authority of God *"...but the woman is the glory of man."* The woman represents or perfects (completes) the glory of God in the man and that is the reason we have to walk as godly women.

The man is the authority and glory of God in the earth—whether you like it or not that is by God's design. I know that some women wish it were different. He created us, we did not create ourselves, therefore, we must walk according to His instruction.

Proverbs 12:4 indicates that a woman is a crown to her husband if she is full of strength in her mind and body, walking according to the Word of God, being filled and full of the Holy Spirit. A woman who is half full of the Spirit and running out, tired, and barely making it is not a crown to her husband. But a woman who has life, and can encourage him—uplift him, meet his needs, and care for him is the kind of woman God wants because she will be the completion of the glory of God in him.

The second part of that Scripture says, *"...but she that maketh ashamed..."* which means she does not honor her husband. If she does not honor him, then she *"...is as rottenness in his bones."* Something that is "rotten or corrodes, makes weak, unsound, his substance and his strength."

"Every wise woman buildeth her house, but the foolish plucketh it down with her hands." (Proverbs 14:1)

When it talks about building here it is mainly talking about the infrastructure of the house. This speaks of what actually lies beneath or below that which you see—the foundation. A wise woman will get an understanding from God of the things that make up a strong home and then work diligently to make sure the main ingredients are in place. A wise woman will see her home going in a certain ungodly direction and use her godly influence to steer it back on course.

Contrary to the behavior of a wise woman, a foolish woman will just haphazardly go from day to day responding to her unfounded whims and desires. She is insensitive to the will of God for her home and is not conscience of the destruction her action will ultimately cause.

It is not so much the disposition of women when things are going well, it is how they act and respond during difficult times that determine whether they build their house or tear it down. It is the right response at the right time that determines the success of anything, including marriage.

Remember, the beginning of wisdom is to fear the Lord and trust in Him. Again, you can develop that

GOD Needs More Annas

trust by spending time with Him. In walking according to His Word when you are in trials, tribulations, persecutions, and difficult circumstances, it will become eminently evident that God's Word is true. You can stand on God's Word! He will cause you to make the right decision at critical times to drive a sure nail into your marriage to increase its stability.

A wise woman builds her home by doing the things that are necessary to edify her family, community, city, state, nation, and the world. She does things so that her household may grow and prosper. It is up to us to help perfect the man, the glory of God in the man, which in turn will bring about the true woman that God wants us to be. God has called us to be virtuous, not foolish, not adulterous, not whorish, not clamorous—making noise, but wise women.

Proverbs, chapter three, is one of my favorite chapters. I try and read it every day because it talks about a person listening to the Word of God. Proverbs 3:1 says, *"My son (I replace it with daughter, because I am a daughter of the Most High) forget not my law, but let thine heart keep my commandment."* It explains that we are to receive His Word, we are to be teachable, and that we allow the Word to be a part of us, we are to allow our hearts to have understanding.

Proverbs 3: 13-23, tells how we are to view wisdom, we are to think of it as a precious stone, it is more precious than rubies. Wisdom is not to be compared with anything in this world. It precedes this world because by it God established the world. The spirit of wisdom proceeds directly from God; it is the cunningness and craftiness of God; therefore, it is to be highly esteemed. Wisdom tells us to obtain knowledge, apply the knowledge given to us, and finally, get an understanding.

It also states in Proverbs that a wise woman knows God and applies the Word of God to her life, this will cause her to build or erect her house. If her house is built on the Word—the truth, it will not fall, because anything that is built on the Word of God will endure the pressures of life, the tests, trials, and tribulations that life brings.

A foolish woman, on the other hand, is a woman who is self-confident, she believes in her own strength, and ability. You cannot build anything in and of yourself, you must have God in your everyday plan. You must have God as your teacher, as your guide, as the One on the forefront telling you what to do.

In every area of our lives, God wants to show us the way to go. He said, *"...lean not unto thine own understanding..."* (Proverbs 3:5). We are to trust in Him and Him alone. He said if we do that, He will make our pathways straight and plain, we will know exactly where to go, as well as when and how to get there.

A woman who is wise will always acknowledge the Lord, she will always know and recognize that He is her Source. He is her Provider, He shows her the way to go. This is in contrast to the foolish woman who wants to do her own thing, who believes that she can do things in and of herself. Therefore, she doesn't want to listen to anyone and cannot be taught.

As children of God, we must be teachable, because God wants to teach us every day. A wise woman builds her house by acknowledging God and realizing that He is the Lord of her life and He will lead her in the pathway of righteousness.

Proverbs, chapter 31, completely describes a virtuous woman. In this particular passage of Scripture, it states how the virtuous woman is not interested in her needs or desires. Instead, she is interested in seeing that her husband and children's needs are met. She supplies them with clothing during the winter, the summer, the spring, she cooks for them. She instructs her children in the Word of God and in righteousness. She is also a business woman. She buys and sells property so that there will be money to meet other needs for the household. She has servants, which means that she has people under her authority. Her husband delegates authority to her and she delegates authority to others.

What I especially like about this particular passage of Scripture is that a virtuous woman is always busy. She is not idle, nor is she a busybody, concerned about finding out the gossip or what is going on in everybody else's home. She is meeting the needs of her own home and in doing so, she is given great praise. Her husband praises her in the gates and her children praise her, because their needs are being met. A virtuous woman does not complain about her needs going unmet because her needs are being met as she serves her family.

A productive woman is one who is able to produce according to the ability God has given her. None of us can do everything perfectly. God has given talents and abilities to each of us and He says in His Word that He would teach us to profit in every area of our lives. We are to produce good fruit, not bad fruit, not overripe fruit, but good sustaining fruit that will remain. Therefore, you can be productive in every area of your life, but God wants to teach you how to profit and be productive. You must learn these skills through the study of the Word of God.

The main verse I really like which sums it all up regarding the virtuous or holy woman, is Proverbs 31:30. Verse 29 leads in by saying, *"Many daughters have done virtuously, but thou excellest them all. Favor is deceitful and beauty is vain, but a woman that feareth the Lord, she shall be praised."*

It says many daughters or many wives have done virtuously, but this particular woman exceeds them. The reason she does so is because she fears the Lord, she gives reverence to God, He has first place in her life. This woman stands in awe of Him. She realizes that she has a covenant relationship with Him, she has confidence in Him and she trusts Him. Therefore, she can do all these things, because she is led by the Lord. The Lord leads her to the places to buy and sell. The Lord leads her to good bargains. The Lord shows her how to care for her children and she gives all the credit to God. She is praised among all others as a result.

I believe that this is a passage of Scripture that God has placed here as a guide. We may not be able to do all these things at the same time, but wherever we are, we are to take the Word of God and allow it to have first place in our lives. Most importantly, we are to fear the Lord. The Bible says, *"The fear of the Lord is the beginning of wisdom..."* (Proverbs 9:10).

The woman that Proverbs 31 describes was not only virtuous, she was holy which means she was consecrated and sanctified for God. She was also a wise woman, which means that she operated according to God, not man. She had understanding and knowledge, using it as a tool for her to provide the best for her family.

Single and married women are to remain consecrated to God. A married woman is to remain holy because the word holy means "consecrated, dedicated, and sanctified." She does this by staying in constant communication with God through prayer. I know it seems as if I keep reiterating the concept of a prayer life, but it is a must. A consistent prayer life was key to Anna fulfilling her calling. The same is true for you. As you allow the Holy Spirit to flow through you in prayer, you will go through a purging process. The Holy Spirit will cause those things that are not of God to be cut away, and those things that God wants to remain will become a part of your character.

First, a woman must have an inner beauty in order for her outer beauty to truly be meaningful. She must walk in love, walk in the Spirit, manifest the fruit of patience, self-control, temperance, faith, joy and peace. These come from the inner man. If a woman does not take the time to build these characteristics, then she will inevitably lack discretion.

"As a jewel of gold in a swine's snout, so is a fair woman which is without discretion." (Proverbs 11:22)

God declares that His people are to be holy because He is holy, (Leviticus 11:44 & 1 Peter 1:15-16). The Scripture did not say to be holy "just if you are single." We are to show forth the image of God in this life, this world, and this age.

A godly woman is one who has a covenant agreement, a relationship with the Lord Jesus Christ. You cannot be godly unless you have a relationship with God. The Bible says, *"No man can come to me except the Father which hath sent me draw him..."* (John 6:44). So first of all, you must come by acknowledging Jesus Christ as your Savior and the Lord of your Life. Then, because your spirit has been recreated and made alive to God, you have the potential to be a godly person.

It also states in the Bible, which is our blueprint (the guide in which we are to follow), that a woman is to be modest in apparel. This means she does not bring undue attention to herself by the way she dresses. To be modest means you dress appropriately according to your size. Whether you are big, middle sized, or small, you are to dress according to what will look appropriate on you. You are not to wear clothing that is too tight. You are not to wear extremely flashy things that will draw people's attention to you. Instead, you are to present yourself in a modest way—not flamboyant, nor overly dressed for an occasion. Allow the Holy Spirit to teach you how to dress, but you must listen and submit to His teachings. You can look in the mirror and see whether your clothes are fitting you properly.

Your apparel is not the only area in which you should exercise modesty. You need to also be modest in eating by not eating too much, but eating just enough to satisfy your hunger. Your speech should be modest, not loud or boisterous, but speaking in a tone and saying things that will not cause people to look at you as if to say, "What is wrong with you?" Modesty, therefore, can apply to all areas of your life. Modesty shows you how to have self-control, to be temperate and to not exercise extremes.

The latter part of 1 Peter 3:4 says, we are to have *"...a meek and quiet spirit."* That means not being easily angered, mild, patient, comforting, submissive, tamely—when ordered about. These behaviors are not innate, they must be learned. We, as women, have to set the example for the young women and girls. They have to see in our family lives that we respect and reverence our husbands.

Proverbs is a good book, it brings everything in line. As we spend time with God, allowing Him to flow through us and out of us, we can be godly women pleasing in His sight.

In describing woman's purpose, the characteristics of the ungodly and godly woman, and the common day challenges of women flowing in the office of womanhood, gives us understanding as to why God needs more Annas.

Chapter Four
A Woman of Great Character

Let's examine the life of a woman by the name of Anna. I want you to look at the different stages in her life, because truly God desires Annas today.

"And there was one Anna, a prophetess, the daughter of Phanuel, of the tribe of Asher: she was of a great age, and had lived with an husband seven years from her virginity;

And she was a widow of about fourscore and four years, which departed not from the temple, but served God with fastings and prayers night and day.

And she coming in that instant gave thanks likewise unto the Lord, and spake of him to all them that looked for redemption in Jerusalem." (Luke 2:36-38)

Here we find this setting in the temple of God in Jerusalem. Now, Mary and Joseph were there with the baby Jesus and He has been circumcised, on the eighth day, according to the law. According to Mosaic Law, forty days after birth, if it was a male child, the woman was to go to the temple for the ceremony of purification. This is the reason Mary, Joseph, and the newborn Christ were at the temple.

The Bible says, *"...there was one Anna, a prophetess, the daughter of Phanuel,"* which means that was her father's name, meaning, "face or appearance of God." She was of the tribe of Asher, which means "blessed or happy."

The Scripture says that she was of a great age and had lived with her husband seven years from her virginity; this implies that she was a virgin at the time of marriage. That means she was obedient to the Word of God as a child. She was brought up in a godly home because she had the Word of God in her heart and walked in it. God desires that all women remain virgins until they are married.

As mothers, it is God's desires for us to teach our daughters the Word of God which includes virginity. There is a reason God created you and He knows exactly how we are, He has also given us His Word and Spirit. God wants us, as women, to be examples. He wants us to teach the statues of God by precept and example.

We also can see from this particular passage of Scripture that if Anna was a virgin when she got married, she was under the authority of God. As a young girl, she had a relationship with God. She was walking according to the Word of God and she was under the authority of her father. She was under the authority of a man, because that is what God wanted. God desires young girls to be under His authority and the man (the father) in the home, because they provide a covering. I know that some of you are thinking, "Well, I am single with children." But the man of God in your life is your covering, the pastor, the priest; God has designed this.

Even young girls, you too have a will and a purpose in the kingdom of God. God will help you live up to His Word. That is why it is important to have a relationship with God, to spend time with Him in communion, even as a young girl. I tell my two daughters, Rachelle and Laura, all the time, "You must have a prayer time, even if you do not come pray with me, you should have your own prayer time, because God has a purpose and plan for you."

As young girls, God can impress upon your heart His will and purpose for you. We must show to this dying and perverse generation, that truly Jesus is Lord. We do not have to compromise and succumb to the world. You can live a holy life, even as a young girl, because that is what God has ordained for you to do, it is pleasing to Him, and He will reward your obedience.

Luke 2:36-38, says that Anna was a wife to her husband. It said, *"...she lived with her husband seven years."* That wasn't a long time, but I am sure she took care of her husband. Are you aware that the Jewish girls at the age of twelve go through a ceremony similar to what the boys go through? After age twelve, they are considered women and their mothers teach them how to handle the responsibilities of home, a husband, cooking, cleaning, and teaching their children the Word of God. Therefore, it is up to us to do our jobs and God is going to hold us accountable for the training of the young girls. We are to be responsible. He does not want us to be lazy and say, "Well it doesn't matter."

Daily our young girls are going to school and being influenced by the world, this includes the Christian schools, because they do not all believe the Word of God. Not every Christian school is upholding God's standards. This is why God places the emphasis on parents, and particularly the women, because God wants us to walk according to His Word. He wants us to do our job. The world is looking at us and God does not want us to bring shame upon His name. He holds us responsible.

We can gather from Luke 2:36, that young girls married at an early age, maybe between 14 and 18-

years-old. Therefore, if Anna married between these ages and lived with her husband for seven years, then she must have been widowed between the ages of 21 and 25—that is still young. However, Anna had a covenant relationship with her God.

Anna did not allow circumstances and situations, being absent from a physical husband, to keep her from doing what God had planned for her to accomplish. God has a plan, purpose and will for each one of us.

Luke 2:37 says, *"And she was a widow of about fourscore and four years..."* This means she was 84-years old. If you subtract 21 to 25 years from 84, that means she was in the temple somewhere between 59 and 63 years, a widow—no physical husband, but she had a relationship with her God, He sustained her.

Luke 2:37 also says, *"...she departed not from the temple..."* At eighty four years-old, the Scriptures did not say Anna was senile, feeble, or sick. She also had good hearing, she could speak, she was in good health. What kept her? The glory of God in her life, because she had a close relationship with her God. There is nothing like prayer, praying in the Spirit, letting the Spirit of God edify and build you up so that you can be the "woman of God" that He has called you to be.

Don't think that you are going to be a woman of God by attending church or reading your Bible every once in a while. That is not going to get the job done! Anna went through different stages of life; childhood, marriage, and being a widow, but she was still vibrant. She had not retired either. She was working for the Lord.

There is no retirement in God. You will work until your day is done. We must work *"...while it is day, the night cometh, when no man can work"* (John 9:4). This is why it is so important that we complete the work God has called us to do.

We can see by Anna's character that she trusted in, had a love for, and possessed patience to wait on God. She had a lot of years of service in the temple and she did not faint. She was praying and fasting, night and day. The Scripture did not say she went out for a while and said, "Oh I think I'll go out and enjoy the world, I am missing something." She had a relationship with God—she knew the will of God for her life.

God wants us not only to know His will for our lives but to walk in His divine purpose. Anna did away with self, using self-control, she denied herself and was able to spend more time with God—she crucified the flesh. Therefore, she was able to remain a widow—godly woman, holy and acceptable to God.

I am sure there were all kinds of people coming in and out of the temple, but Anna was able to stay in the position God had called her to, that is a godly, holy woman. She was aged, but she was committed to God. She was faithful and steadfast in the faith. "Steadfast" means "loyal, unwavering, not changing, firmly fixed, not moving here, there, and everywhere." Anna was settled, unchangeable, established. She knew her place in God, she was not trying to do other things outside of the will of God.

"For none of us liveth to himself, and no man dieth to himself.

For whether we live, we live unto the Lord; and whether we die, we die unto the Lord: whether we live therefore, or die, we are the Lord's.

For to this end Christ both died, and rose, and revived, that he might be Lord both of the dead and living." (Romans 14:7-9)

Women, just as in the case of Anna, God has called us for a purpose. He drew you to Himself for purpose—not to do your own thing. You were bought with a price for a purpose. Jesus Christ died for the whole world, but the whole world is not walking in the Word of God. We must do our part, because we influence other people.

You may want to crawl up in a corner in isolation, but that is unfitting. No man is an island, we are interdependent, influencing each other to do good or evil. No matter what stage of life Anna was in, she trusted God, she believed God, remaining consistent and devoted to being an active worshipper, praiser, and prayer warrior for God.

CHAPTER FIVE
A Woman Under Authority

As a widow, Anna was under the authority of God and the priest—the man of God in her life. There is divine order in the kingdom of God. I know today why my husband and pastor, Bishop Merritt, enjoys seeing women involved in intercession. He knows that they are praying that the bands of wickedness be loosed, that the captives go free. He doesn't have just any kind of women doing the job, just like Anna was not any kind of woman. She wasn't a loose woman. She was under authority, because God had ordained it to be that way.

God does not like rebellious women. Rebellious women get into trouble, they suffer devastating consequences. However, we can live the life that God wants us to live according to His Word, because His Word is going forth, He said, *"I send my Word to heal and deliver them."*

When you hear the Word, your corresponding actions determine whether you really "heard" the Word. If you respond according to the Word, then you have heard. If you do not, that means you have not "heard" and you are rebellious. Rebellion is sin.

"For rebellion is as the sin of witchcraft, and stubbornness is as iniquity and idolatry..." (1 Samuel 15:23)

So we must come into the divine order that God has prescribed and we see this in the life of Anna.

Luke 2:38, *"And she coming in that instant gave thanks likewise unto the Lord, and spake of him to all them that looked for redemption in Jerusalem."*

It was no coincidence that Anna was there (in the temple) at the same time as Simeon, prophesying concerning the Child. She gave thanks also. It did not say she said to Simeon, "I knew it all the time. God showed me the same thing." Did she say that? No! She gave thanks to God, because she knew her place in the kingdom.

Now God had said through Simeon, to Mary, in Luke 2:35, *"Yea, a sword shall pierce through thy own soul also, that the thoughts of many hearts may be revealed."*

God knew that the child Jesus was going to grow up and cause division and that the hearts of people were really going to be revealed.

As you spend time with the Lord, having communion and fellowship with Him, He is going to show you, by the Holy Spirit, your thoughts and intentions of your heart. If they are not according to the Word of God, then He wants you to align them with His Word. He has given us the Holy Spirit, who is the revealer of truth, the leader, guider into the truth, He shows us things to come, and He is our Comforter, our Helper called alongside. God have made every provision possible so that we can be the godly women He has ordained us to be.

Many people are afraid to spend time with the Lord, because He is going to show them exactly what is in their heart. But do not be afraid, it is only for your good. If you walk according to the Word of God, you are going to be pleasing to Him and blessed. He will promote you. Your heart will be changed, therefore, your life will be changed. That is the reason we know we have the answer for the world. But if we are not doing our part, how can we expect the world to come to us? We must display a transformation—a changed person, in every area of our lives. We must not allow the world to influence how we think, what we say, or what we do.

Some of you are spending too much time watching television. It is a setup to influence you. The programs and commercials are full of subliminal, sexual suggestions. This is a fact. There have been studies that conclusively show that television is not going to help you walk according to the Word of God.

Again, as a married woman, we are to nurture and help perfect the glory of God in the man. Single women, this does not exclude you! The Bible says your affections are supposed to be towards God. That is where your heart should be, not on "Who's looking at me?" or "Where should I go to meet somebody?" or "I have to have someone with me, because I do not want to be alone." You are not alone, if you spend quality time with the Lord, He will show you that you are not alone. He will meet your needs right where you are in life. It does not mean that you are always going to be single, but while you are single, be content. God has a plan and purpose for you in every stage of your life.

In 1 Corinthians 7:34, Paul explains that you can do more for God while you are single because you do not have a husband to care for. Once you are married, God wants you to take care of your husband, he comes first. If you are married, you are to try and please your husband, that is number one after ministering to the Lord.

As mature women, we must teach our young women how to please their husbands. It is up to us, it is our responsibility. We do not want them to learn how to please their husbands from the world. Young girls, you are to have a godly husband, not someone you saw walking down the street or who has just recently accepted salvation of Jesus Christ. God wants them to be firmly planted, established, able to take care of you so that you will not have to work. It is about time we start doing what the Word of God tells us to do.

The Holy Spirit has encouraged me to write this book because He knows that we carry great influence by our actions, words, and our lifestyles. Our words and actions must line up with the Word of God. Children can see if our behavior does not line up with the Word. They can see if we are speaking one thing and doing another and you will influence them to do the same. Therefore, it is critical that we submit to authority in order that we may manifest the God-ordained authority for our lives.

Anna, in all stages of her life, was under the influence of God and the man of God in her life. She discerned the will of God for her life. She gave thanks to the Lord, and therefore, she was among one of the first women to proclaim that the Messiah, the redeemer of Israel had come. Yes, there was a woman there. Jesus was just a baby. Therefore, Anna had not seen His works, she did not hear His Word. Yet, because she had a relationship with her God, she knew from the Spirit of God, that what Simeon was saying was true.

God wants you to be knowledgeable, not naïve. God wants you to be informed, enlightened, in accordance to His way and His Word not in darkness. Anna was able to have the title of prophetess because of her relationship with God. She was a female preacher— proclaiming the truth. She did not start off that way, but because God saw that she was faithful, committed, willing to submit to authority (divine order), she was called and ordained by Him; this caused her impeccable lifestyle of godliness to be recorded in the Gospel. She received this title by God because of her character. After the death of Anna's husband, she did not begin living by her own agenda, because she already (prior to marriage) had an intimate relationship with God. She remained under the authority of the man of God.

CHAPTER SIX
A Woman of Prayer

Developing a prayer life does not mean you cannot continue with life's everyday routines (careers, housework, errands, etc.). It simply means that you do not use these as excuses to avoid spending time with the Holy Spirit daily.

As I studied Anna, I found out that her name means, "grace—favor." The Lord said to me, "Yes, Anna was praying, crying out to Me." Even though it is said that the 400 years between Malachi and Matthew were silent years, they were not because women, like Anna, were there crying out to God, breaking down strongholds, so that Jesus would come into the world.

So "Grace—Anna" was praying that He would allow the dispensation of grace to come. Now we must do our part, because Jesus is coming back again. Anna was able to see the physical manifestation of her prayers. She did not give up in those sixty long years of praying in the temple, without knowing who she was actually praying for. Do not give up! God says, "Don't give up!" He says, "Stand firm, be steadfast in the faith, allow the Holy Spirit to flow out of you, so that you can be the witness unto this world."

Our God is a God of purpose, plan, and objectivity. He will cause things to be manifested to you. I do believe we are going to see who we have been praying about. He is going to reward us for our diligence and labor. Our labor is not in vain.

1 Corinthians 15:58 says: *"Therefore, my beloved brethren, be ye steadfast, unmovable, always abounding in the work of the Lord, for as much as ye know that your labor is not in vain in the Lord."*

No matter how old you are, and no matter what your status in life—single, married, or widowed, your relationship with God determines how you are going to influence others. It will determine whether you are going to influence them for the kingdom of God or for the world. You cannot have one foot in and the other out. They must both be firmly planted—unmovable, steadfast, because God has a will and a plan for you. You are precious to God. Again, He sought you to come out from the man, so that you could help complete the glory of God in the man. I pray that the Holy Spirit will reveal this to you.

I believe Anna's success as a true woman of God was directly related to her prayer life, especially after the loss of her husband. She had an intimate relationship with the Lord Jesus Christ and she allowed the Holy Spirit to flow through her so that she could manifest the perfect will of God in her life.

In Isaiah 48:17 it says, *"Thus saith the Lord, thy Redeemer, the Holy One of Israel; I am the Lord thy God which teacheth thee to profit, which leadeth thee by the way that thou shouldest go."*

The word profit means: "To gain, to be benefitted, to be valuable, to ascend, to be useful." We must realize that as women, God wants us to be useful and productive in this lifetime. Prayer caused Anna to profit and be useful, having favor with God as well as man. Remember, she was a prophetess and prayer warrior. In order to be the holy women God has caused us to be, prayer must be an important part of our lifestyles.

King David was said to be a man after God's own heart. We know that he continuously prayed, *"Search me O God and know my heart, try me and know my thoughts: And see if there is any wicked way in me and lead me to life everlasting"* (Psalm 139:23).

In order for us to have the heartbeat of God, it is going to take spending some quality time in prayer. The heartbeat of God is not something you obtain at salvation, but it must be developed. Women, there are no shortcuts, we must develop a prayer life and it only comes by daily spending time with God.

In Luke 18:9-14, Jesus gives a parable concerning two men's prayer lives. Now in this passage of Scripture, both men went into the temple or place of worship and both had the same objective—which was to pray.

Note, Jesus also stated the men's position or status in life, one was a Pharisee and the other a publican. A Pharisee was a man belonging to one of the Jewish religious sects of that day. The word Pharisee means, "separated one."

The Pharisees were noted for separating themselves from the sinners or heathens. They upheld the traditions and were very technical when it came to the Mosaic Law. They were very particular in dealing with the outward details such as the washing of hands before ceremonies or feasts, instead of the washing of the inward man. They were lovers of display and thrived off of being seen. Whatever they did, they wanted it to be a widely publicized display.

Jesus often referred to the Pharisees as "hypocrites" because they were always quick to point out others' wrongs, but presented themselves as perfect. They concentrated on the outward appearance of man and religion rather that the inward development of a man's spirit.

On the other hand, the publican was a Jewish tax collector. Many publicans during this time were involved in extortion or robbing people of the money they paid in taxes. The publicans were classed with the lowest of sinners and were compared with the heathen in Scripture; they were intensively hated by the people.

You can read, however, how the Pharisee in his prayer spoke to God about not being as the sinner or like "this publican." He talked about how he fasted and gave tithes, denoting how religious he was. What he was really saying was "God I expect you to answer my prayer because I am worthy of the petitions I make to you, because I do good works." He was praying as though God answers our prayers based on the good works that we do, implying that God was indebted to him.

The publican, however, came to God in great humility, knowing he was unworthy, confessing that he was a sinner and asking for mercy and grace. Note Jesus' reply: He says that the publican left the temple justified rather than the Pharisee.

As women, we must be careful, not to lead the Pharisee type of prayer life or character, especially in the place of worship. God has a divine order, and it is not His will that we go outside or above the man of God's authority in this area. Remember, the Bible says that we are to have *"…a meek and quiet spirit…"* (1 Peter 3:4). This is not to say that women should not pray in the church, but there is to be order regarding when and how we pray.

A Woman of Faith

Anna was also a woman of faith, which is directly related to having a successful prayer life. Faith is recognizing and committing ourselves, situations, and circumstances to the faithfulness of God.

In Hebrews 11:6, according to the Living Bible it says, *"You can never please God without faith, without depending on Him. Anyone who wants to come to God must believe that there is a God—that He exists—and that He rewards those who sincerely look and seek for Him."*

Your faith is quickened or made active and alive in prayer. Prayer is the indicator of the spiritual condition of your heart. I read in a book that prayer is to the spirit of man, what breath is to body. In other words, you cannot survive without it.

We can assume that if Anna was a prophetess, declaring what thus saith the Lord, she had to be in close fellowship and communion with Him. Although, you may not be a prophetess, you still need a prayer life so that you may carry out the perfect will of God in your life.

CHAPTER SEVEN
A Woman of Humility

We must also be careful not to be hypocrites, because it hinders prayers. As women, we tend to be more detail-oriented than men, which in and of itself this is not wrong. The problem comes when we allow the devil to use this as an opportunity to nit-pick or finger-point at our spouses or other men. Again, a successful prayer life should eliminate this problem. When we read about Anna, the Bible says that she prayed and fasted continually, not having time for menial things.

Because there are more women in the Body of Christ than men, we are generally characterized as the ones who are always in church, fasting and praying. It is important that we not fall into pride. It does not matter what your status in society is—blue or white-collar worker, entrepreneur or housewife, as a woman of God you are to have your own prayer life.

To utilize her gift as a prophetess to the glory of God, Anna had to be in fellowship with the Holy Spirit, who teaches us how to maintain these gifts and not bring shame to the Father's name.

The latter part of James 4:6 reads, *"God resists the proud, but He giveth grace to the humble (the one who takes the low estate, who realizes that he has a need for God)."*

Anna's favor with God and man or her position as a prophetess, was not acquired because she prayed and fasted. As children of God we ought to always pray, but Anna acquired her position by the mercy and grace of God. Because Anna was a woman of prayer and faith, she did not fear life after the death of her husband. She realized that God was her Source, He was her Husband and Covering, she operated in true humility towards God and man. God opposes those who think they can make it on their own, without the help of their Creator, Provider and the Supreme Authority over the earth, the Owner of everything in it.

Anna realized, and so must we, that it is a privilege to pray to a living God. In prayer, we develop and establish a close relationship with God. In prayer, we recognize and acknowledge our need for a Supreme and Higher Authority in our lives. In prayer, we admit the need for a complete dependence on the Father to lead, direct, guide, and make straight our paths.

Anna was a perfect example of someone who obeyed Proverbs 3:5-6, which reads this way in the Amplified Bible, *"Lean on, trust and be confident in the Lord with all your heart and mind and do not rely on your own insight or understanding. In all your ways, know, recognize, and acknowledge Him, and He will direct, and make straight and plain your paths."*

In the Living Bible Proverbs 3:5-6 reads, *"If you want favor with both God and man, and a reputation for good judgement and common sense, then trust the Lord completely; don't ever trust yourself. In everything you do, not some of the things, not a few of them, but in everything you do put God first, and He will direct you and crown your efforts with success."*

CHAPTER EIGHT
A Woman of Persistence and Reverence

Luke 2:37 says Anna *"... departed not from the temple, but served God with fastings and prayers night and day."* This implies that she was persistent with her prayers.

In Matthew 7:7-11, we find out that prayer involves continual asking, seeking, and knocking. In the Amplified Bible it reads, *"Keep on asking and it will be given you; keep on seeking and you will find; keep on knocking (reverently) and the door will be opened to you."*

Maintaining reverence in our prayer lives is especially important in relation to persistence, because it demands that no matter how many times you have to knock, you do not forget Who you are appealing to. When you know the will of God (His will is revealed in His Word) regarding a need, you ask in faith and the manifestation comes because you have asked according to His will.

Prayer is seeking the face of God concerning His will, desires, directions, thoughts, and ways as it pertains to situations, individuals, or yourself. When you know God's revealed will for a situation or circumstance, yet you find a closed door, you are to continue to knock until the door is opened.

Anna was evidently persistent in prayer, because the Bible said, she was in the temple, *"...continually, day and night..."* I believe persistency is a tool that God uses to see if we are truly living by faith.

Jesus also talked about persistency in prayer in Luke 11:5-9. According to the Living Bible, Jesus said to His disciples:

"Then, teaching them more about prayer, he used this illustration: "Suppose you went to a friend's house at midnight, wanting to borrow three loaves of bread. You would shout up to him, 'A friend of mine has just arrived for a visit and I've nothing to give him to eat.'

He would call down from his bedroom, 'Please don't ask me to get up. The door is locked for the night and we are all in bed. I just can't help you this time.'

But I'll tell you this—though he won't do it as a friend, if you keep knocking long enough, he will get up and give you everything you want—just because of your persistence.

And so it is with prayer—keep on asking and you will keep on getting; keep on looking and you will keep on finding; knock and the door will be opened.'"

If Anna had such success in her prayer life without the Holy Spirit, how much more successful should the New Testament Church's prayer lives be? After the resurrection of Jesus and the experience on the day of Pentecost, the disciple's prayer lives changed tremendously.

Before Jesus' death, the disciples slept while Jesus prayed in the garden. Because they were trying to pray within themselves or in the flesh, Jesus inquired, *"...Could you not pray one hour...?"* Once you are filled with the Holy Spirit, He is to have complete control of your spirit man.

If we, as women of God, would begin to walk in this revelation, we will have the results of Acts 1:14, every time we come together. Note that they were not chatting, socializing, or coming together to be seen, they were praying—asking, seeking, and knocking. The Church began with old fashion prayer meetings— revivals, birthing things in the Spirit.

In Acts 2:42, we see that the believers continued in the apostle's doctrine after the Holy Spirit came. They devoted themselves daily to the instruction of the apostles. The believers had fellowship with each other, partaking of the Lord's Supper and praying.

Another place in Scripture where we see believers praying continuously is in Acts, chapter 12. We read that King Herod had Peter and James beaten and imprisoned. Eventually James was killed, the first of the 12 to be martyred.

When Herod saw that it pleased the Jews for him to mistreat believers, he put Peter in prison. However, while Peter was in prison, it reads in verse 5, *"...but prayer was made without ceasing of the church unto God for him."* The Church was asking, seeking, and knocking not to the king, but to the King of kings. They were not protesting and marching up and down in front of the prison, they are not burning the prison, but they were assembled together on their hands and knees before God so that He would intervene in Peter's behalf.

Scripture instructs us to pray without ceasing, to pray in all places—anywhere we can be alone with God. However, we are also to pray as a corporate body. For when we pray, the Holy Spirit working in us both the will and the purpose of God.

Not only are we to pray for a change in our circumstances, situations, troubles, illnesses, and afflictions, but we are to be changed, the fruit of the

Spirit is to be more evident in our lives. This is one of the main reasons we need to pray, so that the Holy Spirit can cause our lives to be more complete, developing to full maturity, to the stature that God the Father desires. When this happens, we will begin to see more true prophetesses in the church, more Annas will arise.

In Luke, chapter 18, Jesus spoke a parable to the disciples explaining that they were to always pray and not faint. In this parable, Jesus speaks of an unjust judge who did not fear God or man.

According to the Living Bible, Luke 18:2-5 reads, *"There was a city judge," he said, "a very godless man who had great contempt for everyone. ³A widow of that city came to him frequently to appeal for justice against a man who had harmed her. ⁴⁻⁵ The judge ignored her for a while, but eventually she got on his nerves.*

"'I fear neither God nor man,' he said to himself, 'but this woman bothers me. I'm going to see that she gets justice, for she is wearing me out with her constant coming!'"

Then the Lord said, "If even an evil judge can be worn down like that, don't you think that God will surely give justice to the people who plead with Him day and night (such as Anna)?" He will answer them quickly. But the question is when He, the Messiah returns, how many will He find faithful and praying? The Almighty God, the righteous Judge, the Deliverer, and Redeemer is looking for faithful women of God, like Anna.

CHAPTER NINE
God Seeks More Annas

The Living Bible says in 2 Chronicles 16:9, *"For the eyes of the Lord run to and fro throughout the whole earth, to show Himself strong in the behalf of them whose heart is perfect, whole, and complete towards Him."*

In these last days, God want us to understand that we were created for His glory, we must realize that God wants to use women now, and He always has. However, you will not be used if your heart—the real you—is not perfect and upright in His sight.

2 Chronicles, chapter 14, begins the account of King Asa's reign. In verse two it reads, *"And Asa did that which was good and right in the eyes of the Lord his God,"* *it goes on to say that King Asa's reign was successful for ten years, in which he did what was right, therefore, he and the people of God experienced peace. When he had to go to war, they were victorious because he called on the world's greatest "military strategist."*

In the fifteenth year of his reign (15:10), King Asa and the people entered into a covenant—to seek the Lord, the God of their fathers, with all their heart and soul. They sought the Lord wholeheartedly, continuously, in and out of season. As a result of their commitment, King Asa and the people of Judah had peace until King Asa's thirty-fifth year—twenty years of peace and prosperity. However, King Asa began to hire foreign or heathen troops, according to 2 Chronicles, chapter sixteen, implying that he no longer needed or trusted God to deliver him and the people of Judah.

In verses 7-10, we find out that King Asa was so angry with the prophet because of the word he had given him that he put the man of God in prison. He also saw to it that some of God's people were brutally oppressed. King Asa's disobedience and rebellion eventually resulted in bodily affliction, of which time he still refused to seek the Lord of help, he sought the aid of the physicians instead. King Asa, like a lot of us, did not consistently seek the Lord for help. He refused to seek the Lord or repent, thereby dying in his affliction.

In this decade, of mass communication—Christian radio, TV, books, tapes, and cd's, it is crucial that we know the Lord for ourselves. These helps are fine if they are being used to assist you in a more in-depth study and understanding of God's Word, but they cannot become a substitute for your personal relationship with Jesus.

We, unlike King Asa, must not become comfortable in our walk with Christ. We, like Anna, must continue in hunger and thirst for righteousness. When we do this, we are recognizing that there is a need for God.

I believe that consistency is a key to a successful walk with Christ. You must keep on asking. You must keep on seeking. You must keep on seeking. You must keep on knocking, because when you do, you are acknowledging your dependence and trust in your God—Creator, Provider, and Source. James says, *"...ye have not, because ye ask not. Ye ask and receive not, because ye ask amiss."* How do you suppose Anna was able to retain her joy, which kept her busy for God after the death of her husband?

Jesus told the disciples in John that if they ask the Father anything in His name they would receive and their cup of joy would overflow and be complete (John 16:24). Anyone who has prayed and received assurance from God that He has heard their request, can only experience joy, because they know, that they know, that they know.

In Psalms, chapter thirty-four, David talks about the Lord hearing the cry of the righteous. In verses four and six he says, *"I sought the Lord and He heard me and delivered me from all my fears... This poor man cried, and the Lord heard him, and saved him out of all his troubles."*

Verse 15 then goes on to explain that, *"The eyes of the Lord are upon the righteous, and his ears are open unto their cry."* The entire thirty-forth division of Psalms speaks of how the Lord delivers or saves and redeems those who seek and trust Him. Whenever you see a verb in the present tense, such as ask, seek, knock, trust, etc., this implies an on-going action. You are to never stop. Continuous prayer will deliver you out of all, not some of your troubles.

As women, we must realize that we are complete in God not man. I believe that this is the main reason so many marriages, even in the Body Christ, end in divorce, because women have unrealistic expectations concerning the purpose of their mate and marriage.

Life does not become so much easier or more comfortable after you are married. Do yourself a favor if you are single and believing God for a mate, ask God to show you the true intentions of your heart. Make sure that you are not marrying for carnal or un-Biblical reasons. Make sure you have a prayer life and an intimate relationship with Jesus before you marry and be honest. If you do not have these things now, do not be deceived into thinking that you are going to develop them after you are married. This is what the devil tells women, but he is a liar. There is no truth in him.

Ask yourself, "Would I remain faithful to God, if I were to lose my husband or if he became totally disabled?" These types of questions will allow the Holy Spirit to show you what is really in your heart, because you don't know. I wonder how many of us would have continued to pray and fast in the temple, night and day, after the death of our mate?

As women, we need wisdom on how to carry ourselves, even how to minister to our husbands. By developing a prayer life, we open the treasures of God's wisdom—His ability to comprehend and insight into His purposes for our life. We are to praise wisdom highly and exalt her because she (wisdom), in return will exalt and promote us.

In James 1:5-8, it says that if we lack wisdom, we are to ask for it, in faith. God's wisdom comes from above and is pure, undefiled, full of compassion and good fruit; it is wholehearted, straightforward, impartial and free from doubt.

I believe that the primary reason we must have a prayer life is because it is a sin not to have one. Sin has a high price that most of us are not willing to pay, nor can we afford to.

In this decade, I believe that we must return to the basics and remain there. I am not saying we do not need new and fresh revelation from God, because we do. However, God does not give revelation for you to dismiss the basics. God shares with individuals things that He wants shared with the Body of Christ, but the purpose of this book is to remind you, as women, that you have a unique responsibility in the earth and you cannot fulfill it is you have not mastered the basics.

In 1 Samuel 12, the man of God, the prophet who had the word of the Lord in his mouth, is speaking to the children of Israel. He said to them, if they would serve the Lord and obey His voice and not rebel against His commandments, that they and the king over them would continue to follow the Lord their God.

"Moreover as for me, God forbid that I should sin against the Lord in ceasing to pray for you: but I will teach you the good and right way, only fear the Lord, and serve Him in truth with all your heart, for consider how great things he hath done for you." (1 Samuel 12:23)

The prophet Samuel is admonishing them to continue asking and seeking. One of the most valuable reasons for prayer is that sinners—those without God, those who do not have fellowship with the Father, can be saved when they pray in faith.

According to Romans 10:9-14, the sinner must first hear the gospel—the death, burial, and resurrection of Jesus Christ, and understand its significance to convert.

Let's dissect verse 13, *"For whosoever (which means any person whatsoever) shall call (Webster's definition of call is, "to say especially in a loud voice, or call out; to ask to come; to appeal to," which means you have got to open your mouth) upon the name of the Lord shall be saved (which means of material and temporal deliverance from danger, suffering; it also includes from illness, being made whole)."* In other words, spiritual and eternal salvation is granted immediately by God to those who believe on the Lord Jesus Christ. It means that someone's salvation could be depending on our consistent prayers.

Anna was an intercessor. She was not in the temple night and day, praying for her own needs, but as a result of her obedience, all her needs were met. God the Father, God the Son, and God the Holy Spirit, separate personalities and yet one God, has made every provision available for you to enjoy a successful life here on earth and in the world to come.

Everything has been completed, so that each one of us has the opportunity to experience fellowship with our Creator.

I believe what kept Anna praying was God's faithfulness in continuing to answer her prayers. The Word of God is filled with answered prayers. We are commanded to pray and God has promised to answer the righteous. God says in Jeremiah 1:12, *"...I will hasten (or am watching over) my word to perform it."* Anna's persistency had to be based on her past experiences with God. His Word had to be an integral part of her life. Just as we depend on physical food in the natural for survival, so we must rely on the Word of God for spiritual survival.

As in the days of Anna, we face another critical time in history—the second coming of the Lord Jesus Christ. The call is going forth in the earth for those holy, steadfast, and persistent women who will stand in the gap, paving the way for His return. God needs some wombs in the spirit to birth the things in the earth that are necessary for the end to come. God need more Annas, those who will submit to the authority He has ordained in the earth. However, submission is an attitude of the heart.

CHAPTER TEN
Submission – An Attitude of the Heart

Women must realize that submission is an attitude of the heart, it takes the Holy Spirit to work it in you. Proverbs 4:23 says, *"Keep thy heart with all diligence; for out of it are the issues of life."* Those who do not understand God's Word, view submission as oppression. Oppression means, "being burdened, having heavy and weary feeling of the body of mind." The whole issue of submission can be burdensome if the wife takes the point of view that "This is something that I really would rather not do."

When the Bible talks about the wives submitting to their own husbands in Ephesians 5:22, the word "submission," means "to set in array under," meaning you are under authority. The way women are taught now it seems as if they either want to be on top or by themselves. They want to prove to the world that they can be equal to men. On the contrary, if they are in the Body of Christ, just having a relationship with Jesus will cause them to realize that they have a certain place in the plan of God, and have nothing to prove. Wives are to submit and not view it from negative perspective, but rather, receiving their role as positive because this is what God has ordained.

"Humble yourselves therefore under the mighty hand of God, that he may exalt you in due time: Casting all your care upon him; for he careth for you." (1 Peter 5:6-7)

If women would humble themselves to the Word, then submission would not be dreadfully looked upon. The problem is that women who do not submit are generally rebellious. This is also true for single women who choose not to submit to their spiritual covering (authority) of church leadership. A woman is to meet the needs of and be suitable for her husband. She is to do it willingly, lovingly, not begrudgingly, and not of necessity, but because this is God's ordained plan.

Mothers need to teach their daughters about their role in the home, and what it means to be a woman, while there are yet young. If mothers would teach their daughters how to care for a mate, and submit to the husband by precept and example, then I don't think that submission would be a problem.

The glory of God, His ordained will and purpose is to be revealed in the human family. Women, you need to realize that you are a part of God's plan and that you can flow with God by your behavior, speech, and the way you treat your husband. You not only can flow with God, but you can help the man become all that he is in God. Therefore, as a woman, you help to complete the ordained plan of God and it cannot be done without you. Through your submitting to the Word of God, and your own husband, you help complete God's original plan before sin entered into humanity. Your role is so critical because you have the key to unlock your family's destiny.

The woman helps the man to actualize his maximized potential in this earth. If women would only realize that God uses them to bring about His plan and purpose in the earth! Women's submission to authority brings glory, honor, and praise **to God** in the earth. When we are submissive to God, it brings **Him** glory. Women are to submit to their husbands **as unto the Lord**, so that **the glory of God in the man** can be manifested, which is one of the primary reasons for God ordaining the family.

"Therefore, shall a man leave his father and his mother and shall cleave unto his wife and they shall be one flesh." (Genesis 2:24)

The Scripture depicts the institution of marriage as neither party belonging to themselves. The husband does not belong to himself, neither does the wife belong to herself, but they belong to each other. Their bodies are no longer their own. They are to become one flesh because God has ordained it to be this way.

The Bible also says, *"...one chase a thousand, and two put ten thousand to flight..."* (Deuteronomy 32:30). The institution of marriage provides a husband and wife with an awesome power in prayer. The Bible explains that if there is any wrath between them, that they are not to *"... let the sun go down..."* without settling it (Ephesians 4:26). This is because of that awesome power they possess in prayer, if they are in agreement. If they can speak the same things, be of the same judgement, be on one accord, then there is nothing that they cannot accomplish.

People do not realize that when they are in agreement, they can achieve so much more as opposed to when they are in disagreement. Therefore, a wife cannot have her own agenda and a husband cannot really have his own agenda, but there are certain responsibilities that God will give to the husband in order for them to function as the family that God has ordained. This is why the wife should be a submissive helper, suitable in order for God's plan to be complete in that family.

I believe that God is the Creator, He knows everything from the beginning to the end and that we are not on this earth without purpose. We are here to fulfill God's plan and His purpose, which is why each family must do their part. A wife cannot do her own thing. She must be governed by the broad picture as opposed to her selfish desires. She cannot say, *"Well, this is my own money, or I am going to do this regardless of what you say."* There needs to be agreement in marriage because productivity is the result when there is agreement. According to Amos 3:3, you cannot walk together unless you agree: *"Can two walk together, except they be agreed?"* So, if you are going to be married, then you must act like you are married, you cannot operate independently of your spouse.

Very often it is hard for two individuals to come together because they are so accustomed to their independence. Therefore, when they come together it takes work. To be one flesh is a result of a lot of tedious work on the part of a couple because it does not just involve being one physically. It takes the two of them taking time to talk, pray, and set goals together—just the two of them. Then, as the children are born, they must continue to do the same thing so that the children will honor God and be pleasing to Him.

There is no such thing as the husband giving 50% and the wife giving 50%, the marriage covenant takes giving of yourself completely—no percentages. God does not recognize percentages in His Word; He says, *"... the two shall become one flesh,"* a new unit have been formed, a new family. The inception of a family does not involve children, even though some individuals may enter a relationship with children from a former relationship. A family begins with the husband and wife. God knows exactly what He wants, so we must be willing to let Him be God, letting Him teach, train, and demonstrate to us what each family should become.

If women do not submit to the headship of their husbands as it is written in the Word of God, then they are not walking in wisdom.

"Forsake her not, and she shall preserve thee: love her, and she shall keep thee.

Wisdom is the principal thing; therefore get wisdom: and with all thy getting get understanding.

Exalt her, and she shall promote thee: she shall bring thee to honour, when thou dost embrace her.

She shall give to thine head an ornament of grace: a crown of glory shall she deliver to thee." (Proverbs 4:6-9)

Therefore, wives who walk in wisdom realize that submission to their husbands is wise because it pleases God. God states that the wife is to submit to her own husband as to the Lord, which means that **she**

submits to her husband as an act of submission to the Lord, because God has ordained order in the human family. It is, however, up to the individual to realize that God's plan is the only plan. Instead, some of us think that we have our own plan that we are supposed to carry out. If a wife fails to adhere to submission, there is still hope because the Holy Spirit is there to cleanse her from unrighteousness and to establish her in right standing with God's truth (1 John 1:9).

A wife who has not been exposed to submission is instructed to, *"... put on the new man, which after God is created in righteousness and true holiness"* (Ephesians 4:24). God has created the human family to know Him and in knowing Him, you will love Him and will not mind keeping His commandments, which includes wives submitting to their husbands. You will then not think of it as oppression.

Submission has to be shown in the home by both parents. There has to be husbands submitting to Christ and wives submitting to husbands. There cannot be just one party doing the submitting, there is supposed to be a dual submission, yet, each one has his or her own role.

If children do not see their parents submitting in a loving relationship, they are not going to want to do it in their own marriages. Submission will be a foreign concept to them because they had not been exposed to it in the marriage setting. But, when the children experience this in the home, they are able to take that which they have seen and say, "This is what God has said we are supposed to do in His Word."

Therefore, when they become of age and get married, they have had a godly example. If they don't have that godly example, they can only do what they have learned in their homes.

It is possible for children who don't see submission in their homes, to come into the knowledge of the Lord Jesus Christ, be filled with the Holy Spirit, and make a change in their lives. They do not have to duplicate their parent's experience. God by His power and their willingness, can break the cycle and establish a new heritage.

To have been reared in a godly home is great, but that is not everyone's testimony. If you have come into the knowledge of the Lord Jesus Christ and if you love Him, you will change in order to please Him. Jesus said, *"If you love me, keep my commandments"* (John 14:15). Therefore, you will take on the image of Jesus Christ, you will want to please the Lord by doing what the Father says, so that you will not do things as the world does them.

The world thinks of submission as something that they should not do, it is every woman for herself. Worldly wisdom says, "Why should I think about what you need? Why should I want to care for your needs?" But that is not what God has said. He said, *"... thou shalt love the Lord thy God with all thy heart, and with all thy soul, and with all thy mind, and with all thy strength..."* (Mark 12:30). Then you are to, *"... love your neighbor as thyself"* (Matthew 19:19). Once you come into covenant relationship with Jesus Christ, you will understand that your husband, children, and family are the ones whose needs must **first** be met. Then, if everything is in order, everything else will flow.

People are accustomed to doing their own thing, so women look at submission as being negative, but it is not. God knows exactly what the human family needs. If people would honor the Lord by doing His will, they would have the most abundant life that they could ever imagine. But it must be done willingly, we must cheerfully want to submit to the Word of God. Wives must want to submit to their husbands, because it is what God has said.

Women must view their roles as *"submitting as **unto the Lord**,"* which will cause them to look beyond the veil of their husband's human flesh and fallibility. Whatever we do, we are to do it as to the Lord, whether it is on our job, in our school, or in the community. We are supposed to be sensitive enough to follow the leading of the Holy Spirit. The Holy Spirit is only going to lead us in what God has already said in His Word. He is not going to do anything else, but lead us into the paths of righteousness, according to the Word of God.

I know that sometimes submission is hard in families where the wife is saved, but the husband is not. It, however, can be done, because God's Word never fails. He said in His word, *"For the unbelieving husband is sanctified by the wife..."* (1 Corinthians 7:14).

The man has to also be taught his role as a husband because if he does not fulfill his role, her needs are not going to be met, which results in her thinking of submission as oppression, suppressing is not submitted to Christ, it makes it difficult for the wife to submit to her husband. As the man is submitted to Christ, he is instructed to keep the Lord's commandments. He is to do what God has said in His Word. God has plainly given us His Word and the Holy Spirit who dwells within us, so that He can help us to do what He has commanded.

Again, God has stated, *"Husbands, love your wives..."* (Ephesians 5:25). This means they are to nourish, cherish, and love them *"... as Christ also loved the*

Church and gave Himself for it," He died for the family. He died for the Church. If a husband would realize that, if he took his role as husband seriously enough and worked to meet the needs of the wife, then she wouldn't be hesitant in submitting to him. The relationship would then be a loving one, not domineering, not one where he has his foot upon her head per se or he is just dragging her behind, but she would be right alongside of him.

If the wife would be meek and quiet, letter the love of God flow through her, demonstrating to her husband that he is the person whom she wants to be with, and take care of him, then she is submitting *"as unto the Lord."* By lovingly taking care of him, cooking for him, washing his clothes, not begrudgingly, but cheerfully she can win him to Christ. Then it is not an act of submitting from a negative point of view, but it is a matter of the wife saying, "I am going to do it God's way, and not my way." The world's way is entirely different from God's way.

We grow up in a world system, with a world's way of looking at things, then the Gospel is preached to us, we become a child of God and God instructs us to renew our minds daily. We must study the Word of God, we must be prayerful, we must *"... watch and pray..."* (Mark 13:13), because *"... your adversary, the devil, as a roaring lion, walketh about seeking whom he may devour ..."* (1 Peter 5:8). Satan will devour anyone who lets him.

Again, I think that the proper perspective and training for males and females stems from being taught in the home while they are young so when it is time for them to get married, they have the right view of what their role is in the home, according to the Word of God.

I cannot over emphasize the importance of women playing a submissive role in the family unit. Therefore, anything outside of submission is rebellion. While a woman is single, she is to be submissive to God and the Word of God which are synonymous. Once she is married, however, she is to continue in the Word, thereby, being submissive to God by being submissive to her husband as to the Lord. You cannot be submissive to God whom you cannot see without being submissive to your husband. Submission does not start once you get married, it simply continues.

Women need to learn their place in society, according to the way God had ordained it. We who are born-again and Spirit-filled in the Body of Christ, have to set the example. We cannot allow the world to speak for us, because they will not express God's perspective, they will give the world's view, the world's system of doing things. Women of God must make a statement to the world by their manner of living, training of children, as well as involvement in the schools and community work. They must articulate God's plan and illustrate it by their lifestyle. In showing the world that there is another way, which is the best way, we can change people's minds and not allow them to misrepresent what we think or how we feel, because they cannot speak for us.

The ERA agenda is not of God. Abortion is wrong. Homosexuality is not an alternative lifestyle, according to the Word of God. Women in the world or in the ERA cannot speak for women of God, because we have a different point of view. We are coming from a different perspective and God expects us, as godly women, to stand up. By this I don't mean you have to protest or picket abortion clinics, but when you are able to speak, take a bold stand for what God says, because His Word is true. If you stand up for truth, you will not fail.

I am sure that women in Anna's day also had their opinion as to what the role of woman was in society. I believe there were also women in Anna's day, as it is now, who defied the laws of God. However, Anna did not allow herself to become distracted by the wisdom of man, but rather chose the things of the Spirit. Such a life of submission to the will of God offers satisfaction that no man can fill. This is why God needs more Annas.

Women of God, will you choose to live an unselfish life that will usher in God's will in the earth? Or, will you go about flowing in the mentality of the worldly women whose behavior denies the power of God and the sound truths revealed in His Word? Choose you this day whom you will serve!

THE INVITATION

Have you accepted Jesus into your heart? If not, today is your day to change your life forever by accepting the gift of salvation.

Pray this simple prayer:

Father,

I thank you for the gift of your Son, Jesus Christ. I ask Jesus to come into my heart now.

I confess with my mouth that Jesus is the Son of God. I believe in my heart that Jesus died for me on the cross, was buried, and was resurrected from the dead.

I repent of sin. I denounce the devil. Jesus take me as your own, live in me from this moment forward.

In Your Name,

Amen.

We believe that you have just taken a step that has changed your life forever.

We want to provide you with **Free Resources** to start you on your journey of faith.

Visit us online at bishopmerrittministries.org and let us know that you have accepted Jesus as your Lord to receive these resources today.

Dear Friend,

We are so grateful that God has given you an opportunity to read this book. We are confident that your life will be changed by the truths you have received.

If you desire to contact our ministry, you may do so by writing or visiting us online at:

Bishop Andrew Merritt Ministries
www.bishopmerrittministries.org

If you desire to send a financial contribution, we will be most thankful for your support.

MAY GOD RICHLY BLESS YOU!

Pastor Viveca C. Merritt

ABOUT THE AUTHOR

Affectionately referred to by the Straight Gate congregation as "Pastor Vickey, Viveca Merritt has served as Co-Pastor of the Straight Gate International Church with her husband, Bishop Andrew Merritt, since her ordination on October 9, 1987. After her ordination, she preached her first sermon on Mother's Day in 1988.

A native of Detroit, Michigan, Pastor Vickey grew up at the Norwest Church of God in Christ, where she was very active in the ministry. She was educated in the Detroit Public School system and graduated from Mumford High School in 1968. She holds a Bachelor of Science in Education (1972) and a Masters of Arts in Child Development (1978), both from Wayne State University.

Viveca met Rev. Andrew Merritt when he ministered at her church in June of 1978. They married on November 4, 1978. She taught in the Detroit Public School system from 1972 to 1984, at which time she left teaching to devote her time to her husband, her family and the ministry.

Bishop Merritt attributes the growth and favor of the Straight Gate Church to the prayers and spiritual fortitude of his wife, Viveca. She has helped to develop many aspects of the ministry and provides spiritual leadership, teaching and guidance to the Women's Ministry. Her ministry to the women of the church, among other teachings, focus on teaching the lifestyle of a virtuous woman, thus inspiring her to write her first book. God Needs More Annas was released in November of 1991.

Pastor Vickey's warm heart and giving spirit are immeasurable and truly treasured within Straight Gate.

In addition to the work of the ministry, she has raised four children: Rachelle (Lorne), Laura (Marc), Jonathan (Tatianna) and David. She also has eight grandchildren: Mariah, Lorne II, Aaron Andrew, Ryan, Lillian, Josiah, Cristina, and Andrew II. She is a woman of virtue and great faith; her household calls her blessed; the church congregation calls her blessed. She continues to teach her children, grandchildren, the women of Straight Gate and loving members every time she comes before the congregation. As her anointed prayers go forth and the power of God is revealed, it is evident that she has an intimate personal relationship with God.

.